To Emily

Merry Christmas, 1981

Love
Mother ♡

Eating Rich

Recipes from America's Wealthiest Families

COMPILED AND EDITED BY
EVELYN BEILENSON

DESIGNED BY
SANDY BAENEN & PATT BAENEN

PETER PAUPER PRESS, INC. WHITE PLAINS · NEW YORK

Contents

Eating Rich

*Recipes
from America's
Wealthiest Families*

COTTON MATHER'S RECIPE FOR PRODUCING HARDY, DURABLE BUSI-NESSMEN was, "Let business engross them." The Rockefellers, Goulds, Carnegies, Fords, and Mellons, the Kennedys, Hunts, and Estée Lauder did just that. Many of these men and women were children of immigrant farmers, mechanics, and small tradesmen. In many cases their formal education was limited, yet their drive and ambition were abundant. Born into families of modest means, they became the founders of such giants as U.S. Steel, Gulf Oil, Standard Oil of New Jersey, and Ford Motor Company.

While amassing their fortunes, did these magnates have time to enjoy the fruits of their labor? Did they eat and live well? The intention of *Eating Rich: Recipes from America's Wealthiest Families* is to give the reader a glimpse of the culinary lifestyles of the rich and famous.

The recipes in italics are original recipes dating back at least 100 years. All other recipes are modern adaptations of old dishes. Much of the information about these families was generously provided by museums and libraries which were once the homes of these great industrialists.

It is the editor's wish that the reader savor the dishes and laugh at the anecdotes associated with these families—whose entrepreneurial power and dynastic fortunes influenced and in many ways enhanced our way of life.

E.L.B.

WILLIAM WALDORF ASTOR

WILLIAM WALDORF ASTOR (1848-1919), son of
John Jacob Astor III, was an intelligent
and ambitious man, although a snob. A desire
for fame led him to venture into politics, at
which he was a failure. His disappointment
resulted in his leaving for England, where he
became a British subject in 1899, and later a
member of the peerage.

In the early 1890's Astor expanded his
New York real estate holdings and built the
Waldorf section of The Waldorf = Astoria on
the corner of Fifth Avenue and 34th Street,
where his mansion had stood. He leased the
property to George Boldt who, with his major
domo Oscar Tschirky, would make the name
Waldorf = Astoria synonymous with luxury,
comfort, and fine food. Before the advent of
The Waldorf = Astoria, eating dinner out in a
hotel dining room was a rarity. Wealthy people
entertained in their beautiful mansions.

Soon after the opening night of the hotel
in 1893 Waldorf Salad was featured on the
menu. Since that time Waldorf Salad has been
served by thousands of Americans and many a
home includes a chafing dish, a novelty item
introduced by the hotel. Chicken à la King,
Lobster Newburg and Welsh Rarebit were all
graciously served piping hot from such
cookware amid the elegant and sumptuous
surroundings of The Waldorf.

Waldorf Salad

4 apples, peeled, cored and diced
¾ cup diced celery
¾ cup mayonnaise
  Juice of half a lemon
¼ cup chopped walnuts
  Lettuce

Place diced apples in a bowl and squeeze lemon over them. Add diced celery and mayonnaise to apples and mix all ingredients thoroughly. Chill mixture and serve on any type of lettuce. Sprinkle with walnuts, and raisins if desired before serving. Serves 6.

Welsh Rarebit

1 tablespoon butter
½ pound aged yellow cheese
⅛ teaspoon salt
⅛ teaspoon mustard
  Dash of cayenne pepper
¼ cup cream
1 egg yolk

Melt the butter in a double boiler or chafing dish. Break cheese into small pieces and add to butter. Then add seasonings to butter and cheese. Stir cream in slowly. When the mixture is hot, remove from the heat and beat in the egg yolk. Serve at once on toast or wafers.

Lobster Newburg

⅓ cup butter, divided
3 tablespoons flour
4 cups half and half
1 teaspoon salt
⅛ teaspoon white pepper
Dash of nutmeg
3 egg yolks, beaten
½ cup sherry or Madeira
1 pound mushrooms, sliced
2 cups cooked and diced lobster

Melt 3 tablespoons butter and blend in the flour. Over low flame, gradually add the half and half, stirring constantly until sauce thickens. Add seasonings. Beat a small amount of the hot sauce into egg yolks. Add egg yolk mixture to remaining sauce, stirring constantly until sauce is smooth and thick. Then add wine and cook for 2 minutes. In another pan, melt remaining butter. Sauté mushrooms, then add lobster and heat thoroughly. Add lobster and mushrooms to the sauce. Cook 2 or 3 minutes longer and serve in heated patty shells or on white rice. Serves 8.

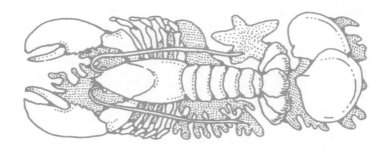

ANDREW CARNEGIE

A NDREW CARNEGIE (1835-1919) came from
Scotland to the United States at age 12, and
started his working life in a Pennsylvania
cotton factory. He advanced rapidly in the
business world, eventually becoming a giant in
the steel, railroad, steamship, iron, and coal
industries, and amassing a fortune.

As one of the richest men in the world,
Carnegie felt an obligation to society, and from
1901 on devoted his life to philanthropic
efforts, which he administered from his
mansion at Fifth Avenue and 91st Street in
New York City (now the Cooper-Hewitt
Museum).

Carnegie refused to be a slave to
convention, and his house was unfashionably
located and architecturally modest for the
time. But the house also had every available
technical device including central air cooling—
a rarity then.

At banquets, held in the formal dining
room, guests signed the tablecloth and their
signatures were later embroidered for
permanence. Carnegie served simple but top
quality food, and only the best Scotch whisky
would do. Among his guests were Mark Twain,
Madame Curie, Booker T. Washington, and
several presidents.

Breakfast was likely to include oatmeal (a
favorite of Carnegie's), kippers, and scrambled
eggs. Other meals probably featured trout and
salmon, which were stocked at his estate in
Scotland. The recipes below would have
pleased his guests.

FRESH GRILLED KIPPERS

Trim heads and tails off the kippers. Brush kippers with melted butter. Place kippers under the broiler for about 3 minutes on each side. Remove and dot with butter. Serve one kipper per person.

TROUT FRIED IN OATMEAL

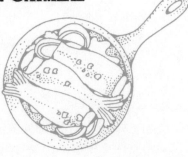

6	trout, cleaned
2	eggs, beaten
	Salt and pepper
1	cup oatmeal
4	tablespoons vegetable oil
1½	ounces butter
2	lemons, sliced
	Parsley

Wipe trout dry with paper towels. Sprinkle the insides with salt. Dip trout in egg. Season oatmeal with salt and pepper. Coat trout with oatmeal. Fry the trout in oil 3 minutes on each side. Place fish on a paper towel to remove excess fat. Dot fish with butter and garnish with lemon slices and parsley. Serves 6.

SMOKED SCOTCH SALMON CANAPES

Slice smoked Scotch salmon across the grain as thin as possible. Place salmon on thin-sliced dark pumpernickel bread which has been cut into triangles. Dust with freshly ground pepper, sprinkle with lemon juice, and top with grated onion, or top with chopped hard-cooked eggs and capers.

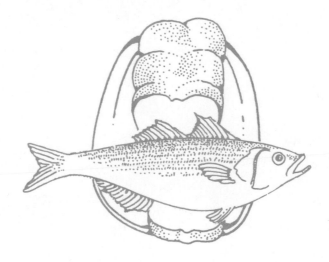

SCOTTISH PORRIDGE

 1   cup old-fashioned rolled oats
3¼ cups cold water
 ½ teaspoon salt

Place rolled oats in a saucepan. Add water, cover, and allow oatmeal to soak overnight. The following day, add salt and bring mixture to a boil, and then simmer for 15-20 minutes, stirring occasionally. Serve immediately with cream, milk, honey or brown sugar, or add salt for the more traditionally-minded.

JAMES DEERING

JAMES DEERING (1859-1925), co-founder and vice-president of International Harvester Company, did not live ostentatiously, as did some of his fellow millionaires in the early 20th Century. Rather, he lived a quiet and simple bachelor life. Possibly this was due in part to the fact that he suffered from pernicious anemia, which could not be effectively treated at the time.

In a departure from this life style, however, Deering did build a magnificent Italian Renaissance-style villa which he named Vizcaya, in Miami, Florida. This house, which he lived in from 1916 to 1925, incorporated every luxury and amenity for entertaining.

Deering only occasionally entertained at night in the banquet hall, usually for a special guest like Ignace Jan Paderewski, the great Polish pianist. He would more likely invite guests to outdoor luncheons in the shaded arcade, following cocktails in the sunny open courtyard.

Food, including vegetables and fruit, was grown on the 180-acre estate, and chickens were provided from the estate's large poultry house. Meals were prepared by the French chef, Monsieur Cazes. More than likely, his recipes featured local pompano, grouper, red snapper, shrimp, Florida lobster and stone crabs. Deering's guests dined sumptuously, although Deering himself, because of poor health, may have been prevented from enjoying M. Cazes' splendid menus.

Baked Red Snapper

4 red snapper fillets, ¾ pound each
½ cup dry white wine
1 tablespoon teriyaki sauce
2 tablespoons butter
   Parsley, chopped
1 lemon

Preheat oven to 400 degrees. Arrange snapper fillets in a shallow baking dish just large enough to hold them without overlapping. Pour wine over fish. Sprinkle fillets with teriyaki sauce and parsley and dot with butter. Bake for 10 minutes or until done. Garnish with lemon slices. Serves 4.

POMPANO BAKED IN TOMATO SAUCE

8 medium-size skinned pompano fillets
2 cups tomato sauce
1 small onion, grated
1 green pepper, diced
2 teaspoons chili sauce
1 teaspoon Worcestershire sauce
½ cup fresh shrimp, peeled and deveined
Salt and pepper to taste

Preheat oven to 400 degrees. Place fillets in an oven-proof baking dish, making sure they do not overlap. Combine remaining ingredients in a saucepan and bring to a boil. Pour sauce over fish and bake for 10 minutes or until done. Serves 4.

FLORIDIAN BAKED CHICKEN IN BUTTER

2 broilers, cut into serving pieces
Seasoned flour
2 eggs, beaten
Bread crumbs
½ pound butter

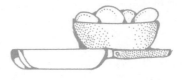

Dip pieces of chicken first in seasoned flour, then in beaten eggs, and last in bread crumbs. Melt butter in baking dish, lay pieces of chicken in melted butter, and bake for 2 hours at 350 degrees, turning chicken once so that both sides are properly browned, and increasing heat to 500 degrees in the last 10 minutes to make chicken crisp. Serves 6.

E.I. du Pont

Eleuthère Irénée du Pont de Nemours (1771-1834), born in Paris, arrived in America with his family at the turn of the 19th Century. He had studied chemistry in France, and was able to develop and manufacture a cheaper yet higher quality gunpowder than was available in the United States. In 1802 he started building powder mills near Wilmington, Delaware, on the Brandywine River, which provided the necessary waterpower. Du Pont sold to both private customers and the Federal government, and the War of 1812 proved very profitable and allowed for the expansion of his milling operation.

Farming had been an important part of du Pont's boyhood in France. His family home on the Brandywine, called Eleutherian Mills, was planted with beautiful gardens of both French and native American origin, and provided food for the family year-round. Du Pont was especially proud of his annual crop of Yankee pumpkins.

Among the notable visitors to his home were the Marquis de Lafayette, Henry Clay, and President James Monroe. Today, this beautiful 200-acre property is a National Historic Landmark known as the Hagley Museum, and includes a restored garden of the 1830's. The following family recipes are from the Hagley Cookbook.

Citrus fruits were not readily available in 19th Century Delaware groceries. The du Pont family, however, could enjoy dishes like lemon butter because they carefully tended their own lemon trees. Originally grown by E. I. du Pont's wife Sophie, "Mama's trees" were always brought indoors in tubs before the first frost.

Lemon Butter

4   *tablespoonfuls lemon juice*
1   *teaspoonful grated rind*
¹/₂ cup sugar
¹/₂ cup flour
1   *cup water*
1   *egg*
1   *teaspoonful butter*
    Few grains salt

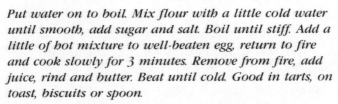

Put water on to boil. Mix flour with a little cold water until smooth, add sugar and salt. Boil until stiff. Add a little of hot mixture to well-beaten egg, return to fire and cook slowly for 3 minutes. Remove from fire, add juice, rind and butter. Beat until cold. Good in tarts, on toast, biscuits or spoon.

A kitchen garden was an absolute necessity to the young French family newly arrived on the Brandywine in 1802. One of E. I. du Pont's greatest concerns, as expressed in letters to his father, was that his children should have fresh fruit and vegetables. There were onions, artichokes, asparagus, beans, cabbage, herbs—all planted in neat rows and kept through the winter in root cellars. This purée recipe was given to Louisa du Pont by her sister-in-law Eleuthera (du Pont) Smith (1806-1876).

Purée d'Oignons (Onions)

*Cut in small pieces 1 dozen or more white onions from
which you have previously removed the tops and roots.
Boil them in milk and water, until perfectly tender,
then put through colander, and put them back in the
saucepan with some salt, pepper, and a piece of butter.
Just before serving put in large tablespoonful of wine.
If the onions are too dry, a little cream may be added.*

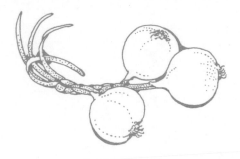

The first chestnut trees planted at
Eleutherian Mills were sent to du Pont by a
friend in France. Chestnuts in hot milk were a
special treat on winter evenings.

Chestnuts as a Vegetable

*Cook one quart Spanish chestnuts 15 minutes. Peel off
skin, put in kettle with enough water to cover. Take ½
package seedless raisins, ½ pound butter, 1 cup brown
sugar. Cook slowly until very tender, about one hour in
double boiler.*

WILLIAM DU PONT, SR.

DUE TO STRAINED FAMILY RELATIONS, William du Pont, Sr. (1855–1928), the fourth richest du Pont and grandson of E.I. du Pont de Nemours, had little to do with the family's chemical and industrial companies. Instead, he organized the Delaware Trust Bank and operated one of the major thoroughbred farms in Virginia.

Much of his life was lived on a magnificent 2,700-acre estate called Montpelier, in Montpelier Station, Virginia. This majestic 18th Century estate had previously been the home of James Madison, the fourth president of the United States.

In 1911 William du Pont organized the Montpelier Supply Company through which he bought produce and merchandise at wholesale and sold to the workers on the estate and to the surrounding population. One could buy all types of hardware, tools, bulk foods, medicaments, and even ice and fruit (which were novelties before World War I). Made with ice from the store and cream from the dairy, homemade handcranked ice cream was a du Pont favorite. Game chickens and yellow squash, both raised on the farm, were also served and enjoyed at the du Pont table.

Vanilla Ice Cream

2 cups milk
1 cup sugar
¼ teaspoon salt
4 cups light cream
4 tablespoons vanilla
7 pounds crushed ice,
 approximately
2 cups rock salt, divided
1 cup cold water

Fill hand cranked container ⅔ full with mixture of milk, sugar, salt, light cream and vanilla. Fill tub around freezer can to level of drain hole with finely crushed ice, layering every few inches with ½ cup rock salt. After tub is filled, add cold water to shorten freezing time. Start cranking by hand until ice melts enough to flow as water through drain hole. Keep adding salt and ice to keep level at drain hole. After 20 minutes of steady cranking mixture should be mushy. Ice cream may then be hardened in freezing compartment of refrigerator. Scrape ice cream from the dasher or let those who have been cranking have the treat of licking the dasher. Makes 2 quarts.

Roasted Game Chicken

Dress, clean and truss chicken. Place it on its back on rack in dripping pan, rub entire surface with salt, sprinkle with pepper and spread breast and legs with butter, rubbed until creamy and mixed with 2 tablespoons flour. Dredge bottom of pan with flour. Place in 450 degree oven and when flour is well browned reduce heat to 350 degrees; then baste.

Continue basting every 10 minutes until chicken is cooked. For basting, use ¼ cup butter, melted in ⅔ cup boiling water, and after this is gone, use fat in pan, and when necessary to prevent flour burning, add 1 cup boiling water.

SAUTEED SUMMER SQUASH

4   cups summer squash
4   tablespoons butter
1   cup chopped onions
    Salt and pepper to taste

Wash and dice squash. Saute onions in butter until they are translucent. Add squash. Salt and pepper squash to taste. Cover pan and cook until tender, stirring occasionally to prevent squash from sticking to pan. Cooking time is approximately 10 minutes. Serves 5.

HENRY MORRISON FLAGLER

THE SON OF A POOR PRESBYTERIAN MINISTER in Hopewell, New York, Henry Morrison Flagler (1830-1913) left home at the age of 14 to seek his fortune, which he did with great success, eventually becoming one of John D. Rockefeller's closest colleagues and helping to organize the Standard Oil Company.

On Flagler's honeymoon with his second wife, he fell in love with Florida, and from 1886 on began to develop its entire East coast into a gigantic resort area. Acquisition of several small railways led to expansion of these lines into the Florida East Coast Railway. Finally, in 1912, he completed the bridges and causeways to Key West.

In 1901 Flagler built in Palm Beach a magnificent home called Whitehall as a wedding present for his third wife, Mary Lily Kenan. Here they entertained graciously, though not always on a grand scale. As Arthur Spalding, the resident organist, wrote: "We had a very simple dinner, but delicious and handsomely served."

On another occasion, the Flaglers gave a more elaborate meal for the Duke of Manchester. The menu is reprinted on the following page.

Dinner given by Mr. Flagler for the Duke of
Manchester ca. 1910

Reception:
Le Caviar Beluga Malossol sur Socle
Crepes Alexis, Le Blini a la Russe
Cuvée Dom Perignon

Premiere Assiette:
Le Poule au Pot Henri IV, La Croute Moelle
Madeira Serial

Deuxieme Assiette:
Le Crabe de l'Atlantique Frais Flambé
Wehlener Sonnenhur

Troisieme Assiette:
Le Caille Pectoralis Cecilia en Gelée
Chassagne Montrachet Marquis de Laquiche

Quatrieme Assiette:
Le Selle d'Agneau roti Lafayette, Sauce Madère
Chateau Lafite Rothschild

Issue de Table:
Les Laitues de Kentucky au Coeur de Palmier,
L'Huile de Noix et Citron

Le Plateau de Fromages:
Stilton de Leicestershire
Brie de Coulomniers

Les Douceurs:
Le Soufflé au Grand Marnier Lapostolle,
Accompagné de son Sabayon Doré
Chateau d'Yquem

Le Café:
Le Café Brulot
Napoleon Fine Champagne

GRAND MARNIER SOUFFLÉ

3 tablespoons butter
3 tablespoons flour
⅛ teaspoon salt
1 cup light cream
½ cup sugar
6 eggs, separated
3 tablespoons Grand Marnier

Preheat oven to 350 degrees. Butter a two-quart soufflé dish generously and dust with sugar. Fit with a 2″ high collar of wax paper, buttered and sugared on the inside.

Melt butter in a small pan. Blend in the flour and salt. Gradually stir in the cream and bring to a boil, stirring until thick. Stir in the sugar to dissolve. Beat in the egg yolks one at a time. Stir in the Grand Marnier. Beat the egg whites until stiff. Stir half the whites into the sauce. Fold in the remaining egg whites.

Pour mixture into the soufflé dish and bake about 40 minutes. Serve immediately with a hot raspberry sauce. Serves 6-8.

Note: Although the American Soufflé is baked 40 minutes at 350 degrees, the French method calls for baking only 30 minutes at 400 degrees.

ZABAGLIONE

6 egg yolks
1 teaspoon vanilla
6 tablespoons brandy
6 tablespoons sugar

Beat egg yolks. Add vanilla, brandy, and sugar. Pour this mixture into a double boiler and beat constantly until it thickens. Pour zabaglione into sherbet glasses and serve warm or chilled. Serves 4.

HENRY FORD

H ENRY FORD (1863-1947) did not invent the automobile. His success derived from his ability to build a car more efficiently, by use of the conveyor belt assembly line, and sell it to the masses at a low price. Between 1908 and 1927, he sold 15 million of his Model T "Tin Lizzies," mostly in a single color—coal black. Ford's use of standardized parts and mass-production techniques revolutionized American industry, as did his introduction in 1914 of the $5 per day minimum wage.

While the assembly line was the great invention of Ford's earlier years, his promotion of the soybean as a food and as a potentially important cash crop became an outstanding achievement of his later life.

During the 30's and early 40's Henry Ford tried to develop palatable foods based on soybeans, although the soybean biscuit was described by one of Ford's secretaries as "the most vile thing ever put into human mouths" and by another employee as "just like eating hay." No one foresaw that the soybean would one day become a basic part of health enthusiasts' diets and a component of many popular food products, plastics and fabrics.

The soybean recipes that follow were often served at Henry Ford's daily roundtable luncheons at the Dearborn Engineering Laboratory.

Nut Bread

1 cup brown sugar
2 cups sour milk
1 teaspoon baking soda
3 teaspoons salt
2½ cups bread flour
1 cup soy bean flour
2½ teaspoons baking powder
1 cup roasted soy beans

Combine sour milk, brown sugar, salt and baking soda. Mix well. Mix soy bean flour, bread flour and baking powder; add to sour milk mixture. Fold in roasted soy beans. Bake in a well-greased and floured pan for forty minutes at 350 degrees.

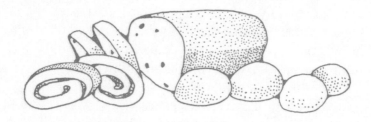

Croquettes

2 cups soy bean cheese
1½ tablespoons butter
1½ tablespoons flour
½ cup milk
1 tablespoon chopped onion
¾ teaspoon salt
¼ teaspoon poultry powder
1 cup bread crumbs
1 egg

Mix all ingredients except egg and bread crumbs and form into croquettes. Dip into beaten egg and roll in crumbs. After drying some, cook in deep fat at 375 degrees for five minutes and drain.

Soy Bean Salad

½ cup raisins
½ cup chopped apple
½ cup boiled soy beans
½ cup chopped celery
　Mayonnaise dressing

Mix ingredients together and serve on a bed of lettuce with a mayonnaise dressing.

Soy Bean Bread

2　cups lukewarm milk
2　yeast cakes
1⅓　cups soy bean flour
3　cups bread flour
3　level teaspoons salt
3　level tablespoons butter or Crisco
3　level tablespoons sugar

Dissolve yeast in lukewarm milk; add soy flour and bread flour, mix a little, then add salt, sugar, and butter or Crisco. Let rise in a warm place. This should take about 1½ hours. Punch down the dough and after 15 minutes mold into 1 large loaf or 2 small loaves weighing about 1 pound 2 ounces each. Let rise until 3 times its size. Bake in an oven at 350 degrees.

Recipes courtesy of Henry Ford Museum & Greenfield Village

HENRY CLAY FRICK

HENRY CLAY FRICK (1849-1919), raised on a farm in southwestern Pennsylvania, had little formal education but was an avid reader, and at an early age became an art collector. As a youth, he worked as a store clerk and at other jobs. At age 21, in partnership with two cousins, he founded Frick and Company to manufacture coke, the fuel used in making steel, and became a millionaire by the age of 30.

Frick continued his rapid rise in industry, becoming chairman of the Carnegie Steel Company and helping J. P. Morgan form the United States Steel Corporation.

In 1913-14 Frick constructed a house at 70th Street and Fifth Avenue in New York City which is now the permanent home of The Frick Collection. He brought Joseph Donon, who trained under the great chef Escoffier, to the United States in 1912 to be his private chef at the Frick residences in New York, Pittsburgh and Pride's Crossing, Massachusetts.

Frick's death occurred 28 days after eating a bad lobster (served by a later chef) which presumably gave him ptomaine poisoning and brought on other fatal complications.

One of the dishes that Chef Donon served the Fricks was a goose and bean casserole, the recipe for which follows.

CASSOULET DE CASTELNAUDARY
(CASSEROLE OF GOOSE AND BEANS)

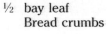

1	young goose	½ bay leaf
1	pound white beans	Bread crumbs
1	garlic sausage	
¼	pound lean salt pork	
2	garlic cloves	
4	onions	
4	cups beef stock	
1	sprig of thyme	
2	sprigs of parsley	
2	tomatoes	

Soak the beans overnight. Cover them with fresh water, add 2 onions and a little salt and pepper, and cook slowly for about 2 hours. The beans should be about three-fourths done.

Have the goose cut into 12 pieces and the garlic sausage into short lengths. Brown both in a little melted butter and transfer them to a *cassoulet,* or shallow earthenware baking dish, which has been rubbed with a cut clove of garlic.

Dice the salt pork, blanch it, and brown it quickly in a skillet. Add the remaining onions, sliced, and the garlic cloves, chopped, and cook until the onions are lightly browned. Sprinkle with 1 teaspoon of flour, and cook, stirring, until the flour is browned. Stir in the beef stock, bring the liquid to a boil, and add the herbs and the tomatoes, peeled and coarsely chopped. Cover the pan and cook the sauce for 20 minutes over low heat.

Drain the beans and spread them over the meat in the *cassoulet.* Pour the sauce over all and bake in a moderate oven (350 degrees f.) for 1 hour. Sprinkle with bread crumbs and return the *cassoulet* to the oven to brown the crumbs.

From The Classic French Cuisine, *by Joseph Donon. Copyright © 1959 by Joseph Donon. Reprinted by permission of Alfred A. Knopf, Inc.*

Modern day methods of handling shellfish help protect the consumer from ptomaine poisoning, and we therefore feel free to include the following two lobster recipes.

FRESH BOILED LOBSTERS

1½ gallons water
⅓ cup salt
6 lobsters (1¼ pounds each)
   Melted butter

Pour water into a lobster pot. Add salt, cover and bring to a boil. Plunge lobsters into pot head first. Cover and simmer for 15 minutes. Drain, crack claws, and serve with melted butter. Serves 6.

LOBSTER THERMIDOR

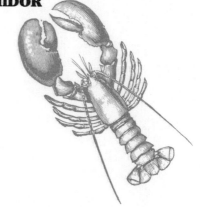

4 small boiled lobsters
8 tablespoons melted butter
4 tablespoons flour
4 cups milk
2 cups sharp cheese, grated
2 egg yolks
2 teaspoons paprika
   Salt and pepper to taste
   Bread crumbs

Cut meat from lobster into small pieces. Blend butter and flour over a low flame. Add milk, stirring constantly until the sauce is smooth. Add cheese, egg yolks, paprika, salt and pepper. Stir continuously until sauce thickens. Add lobster meat to sauce and pour this mixture back into lobster shells or a casserole dish. Cover lobster with bread crumbs which have been browned in butter. Bake in a 350 degree oven for 20 minutes. Serves 4.

J. PAUL GETTY

J. PAUL GETTY (1892–1976) WAS AN OIL FIELD WILDCATTER, an incredibly successful businessman, a writer and an art collector. He entered the oil business, speculating in Oklahoma oil leases, and by age 23 was a millionaire and decided to retire. When his father died in 1930, however, Getty became obliged to reenter the workforce—as president of George F. Getty Incorporated, the family oil firm.

Although Getty became one of the richest men in the world, he was extremely careful with his money. It was not until the ripe old age of 67 that Getty gave up living in inexpensive hotel suites and bought a magnificent mansion outside London called Sutton Place. Here he installed a pay phone so that guests would not take advantage of his hospitality.

On June 30, 1960, in a rare show of extravagance, Getty invited 1200 guests to Sutton Place for a housewarming party. The dinner menu included caviar, consommé, roast veal, giant English strawberries with Devonshire cream, and lobster (which was served afterward as part of a late supper). The cost of the party was high but, ironically, the enormous publicity generated by the party made it a bargain for the Getty companies and their stockholders.

CONSOMMÉ

6 chicken backs
1 pound veal bones
1 pound marrow bones
1 pound lean beef
6 quarts cold water
1 tablespoon vegetable oil
⅓ cup sliced onion
⅓ cup chopped celery
¼ cup coarsely chopped carrots
  Pepper to taste
¼ teaspoon grated nutmeg

Place cleaned chicken backs in soup kettle, with soup bones. Cut beef into small pieces and brown in a hot skillet with marrow from the marrow bones. Add to soup kettle. Add the cold water. Heat quickly to boiling point, skim if a clear soup is desired. Cover, let simmer slowly for 5 hours. Fry the vegetables in oil for 5 minutes. Add vegetables to soup and allow to boil 1 hour longer. Strain and season to taste. When cool, remove fat. Reheat and serve.

Roast Shoulder of Veal

1 4 pound boneless shoulder of veal, rolled and tied
   Salt and pepper to taste
½ pound bacon
3 carrots, chopped coarsely
2 garlic cloves
3 onions, quartered
1 bay leaf
   Pinch of thyme
½ cup butter, melted
1 cup dry white wine
3 tablespoons sour cream

Preheat oven at 300 degrees. Season veal with salt and pepper. Wrap bacon around veal. Place veal in roasting pan and insert meat thermometer in the thickest part of the meat. Place carrots, garlic, onion, bay leaf and thyme around meat. Baste meat frequently with melted butter and wine until meat thermometer registers 170 degrees, about 2 hours. Raise oven temperature to 400 degrees for last half hour. Remove vegetables and juices from the pan and blend in a blender. Add sour cream and blend again. Pour sauce over roast. Reheat in the oven for five minutes. Slice and serve.

Clotted Cream or Devonshire Cream

Allow certified unpasteurized cream to stand in a heatproof dish for 12 hours in the winter and 6 hours in the summer. Place cream over heat. Simmer at a very low temperature never allowing cream to boil. When small rings appear on the surface of the cream the cream has sufficiently scalded. Remove immediately from heat and place in the refrigerator for at least 12 hours. Skim the clotted cream and serve with scones and preserves or with berries.

JAY GOULD

JAY GOULD (1836-1892), born in Roxbury, New York, rose to become one of the richest and most powerful men in the country, despite a childhood of poverty and little formal education. After holding jobs as a blacksmith, clerk, and surveyor, he ventured into other fields, eventually controlling a railroad network that reached almost across the country.

Gould once described himself as "the most hated man in America." His business ethics were questionable, to say the least, and he was the prototype of the "robber baron."

At the height of his power in 1880, Gould purchased Lyndhurst, a Gothic Revival castle on the Hudson situated in Tarrytown, New York. He used the estate as his country retreat until his death from tuberculosis in 1892. After Gould's death, his daughter Helen maintained Lyndhurst for more than four decades. Then his younger daughter Anna, the Duchess of Talleyrand-Perigord, used the estate sporadically in the World War II period, entertaining friends and family as well as servicemen, and thereafter until her death in 1961. From her butler's journal, we have a menu from one of Her Grace's Christmas dinners.

Her Grace

Christmas 1958
Five at 2 P.M.

Assorted olives, celery hearts, carrots &
radishes
Clear Home Made Chicken Consommé
Bouchées of puffed paste

Poached Filet of Sole, White Sauce Supreme
Small puffed patties

Roast Young Turkey, Chef's Stuffing
Giblet gravy
Jellied cranberry mold
Baked sweet potatoes   Green string beans

Salads

Christmas plum pudding
Hard Brandy Sauce
Stewed Pears

ROAST TURKEY

Dress and clean turkey. Rub inside with salt and pepper. Stuff neck cavity. Fasten opening with metal pins. Fill body cavity loosely with stuffing. Rub with butter or make paste of ½ cup butter and ¾ cup flour. Spread over all parts of the turkey.

Place turkey breast side down in open roasting pan to allow juices to run down into breast. Drip pan from broiler may be used if large roaster is not available. Roast uncovered in 300-325 degree oven 15 to 20 minutes per pound, turning turkey over onto back when half done.

Baste at 30-minute intervals with mixture of melted butter and hot water. When breast and legs become light brown, cover with foil. Turkey is done when the meat pulls away from the leg bones.

STUFFING

4   cups dry bread crumbs
1   medium-size onion, chopped
1   teaspoon salt
¼   teaspoon pepper
    Sage to taste
    Parsley, chopped
¼   teaspoon poultry seasoning
⅓   cup butter, melted
    Hot water or stock to moisten

Combine bread, onion, and seasoning. Add butter and sufficient liquid to moisten. Mix gently. Allow 1 cup stuffing for each pound of poultry or game.

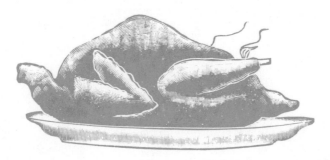

WILLIAM RANDOLPH HEARST

WILLIAM RANDOLPH HEARST (1863-1951) was, at the height of his career, the owner of a communications empire that included 26 newspapers, 16 magazines, 11 radio stations and two movie companies.

This controversial man, for all his business enterprises, alleged "yellow journalism" and political aspirations, will most likely be remembered for his vast art collections and grand estates, particularly San Simeon castle in California.

Here he entertained presidents, movie stars, writers and other famous people. At dinners, guests were seated along 400-year-old wooden convent refectory tables without tablecloths. Silverplate flatware and paper napkins were used. In the center of the table surrounding 17th Century silver candlesticks were home-canned jams, jellies, pickles and relish. Catsup and mustard in grocery-bought jars with prices still attached completed a bizarre hodgepodge of the elegant and the commonplace.

A standing rib roast, or perhaps a turkey or leg of lamb, all from animals raised on the property, was brought into the dining room and served on an English Sheffield serving tray. Quail, pheasant and game hens were cooked on an indoor grill. The recipes below are typical of San Simeon fare.

PRESSED DUCK

Prepare duck for roasting. Have it at room temperature. Place in a very hot oven, 500 degrees. Roast for 12 minutes. Remove from oven. Remove breast from carcass in one piece; place on a warm platter. Keep warm. Remove leg joints from carcass and place carcass in a warm duck press. Press duck, removing all blood and juice from carcass. Strain into a warm dish, and add ½ teaspoon soy sauce, ½ teaspoon Worcestershire sauce, salt and pepper. Pour a small amount of blood and juice around breast on hot platter. Garnish with spiced crab apples and cooked small white onions. Duck for this dish should be slaughtered in a manner so there is no loss of blood.

ROAST PHEASANT

Heat oven to 450 degrees, heat shallow open pan in oven. Tie legs and wings of bird close to the body. Cover breast with slices of salt pork. Tie pork in place. Put bird on its side in warm pan and pour ¼ cup of oil over all. Roast uncovered for 15 minutes. Baste often. Turn bird and repeat. Turn bird on its back and baste and roast 30 minutes, or until done. Serve with bread sauce.

BREAD SAUCE

1 medium onion
2 whole cloves
2 cups milk
  dash cayenne pepper
¼ teaspoon salt
1 cup fresh bread crumbs
1 tablespoon butter or margarine

Stud onion with cloves. Place in saucepan with milk, cayenne pepper, salt. Bring to boil. Simmer about 5 minutes; strain. Add bread crumbs; stir in butter. Use with game birds.

Above recipes reprinted from The Enchanted Hill Cookbook, *by Marjorie Collord and Ann Miller, (Blake Printing & Publishing, Inc., San Luis Obispo, California, 1985).*

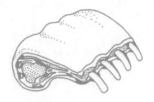

STANDING RIB ROAST

Select a 2- or 3-rib standing rib roast (4 to 5 pounds). Place fat side up in roasting pan; season with salt and pepper and place in 350 degree oven. Do not cover and do not add water.

Allow 18 to 20 minutes per pound for rare roast, 22 to 25 minutes per pound for medium, and 27 to 30 minutes per pound for well-done roasts. Serve with Yorkshire Pudding.

MILTON HERSHEY

A LTHOUGH HERSHEY AND CHOCOLATE are synonymous to most Americans, chocolate did not become an important part of Milton Hershey's life until he was about 40 years old. Before that time, he had tried and failed at several ventures, until he made a success in the manufacture of caramels.

· During a visit to the Chicago World's Fair in 1893 Hershey saw German chocolate-making machinery, purchased it, and had it installed in his Lancaster, Pennsylvania factory. In 1900 he sold the caramel factory for $1 million and devoted himself to making chocolate exclusively. He located his new factory near his birthplace in nearby Derry Township, because it had an ample water supply, fresh milk, and a good labor pool.

The Hershey Chocolate Company was successful not only in this country; it quickly developed into the largest chocolate manufacturer in the world. Milton Hershey used some of his fortune to create a school for orphan boys and also contributed to maintaining local public schools and establishing a tuition-free junior college.

Hershey (1857-1945) was brought up in a Mennonite family, and the following dishes, provided by the Hershey Museum, were probably served frequently in his home.

CHICKEN CORN SOUP

1   3 to 4-pound chicken
1   tablespoon salt
¼   teaspoon pepper
1¾ cups chopped celery
¾   cup chopped onion
2   tablespoons minced parsley
4   cups corn (fresh, canned, or frozen)

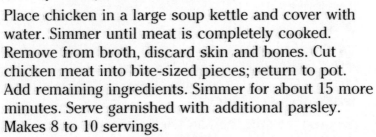

Place chicken in a large soup kettle and cover with water. Simmer until meat is completely cooked. Remove from broth, discard skin and bones. Cut chicken meat into bite-sized pieces; return to pot. Add remaining ingredients. Simmer for about 15 more minutes. Serve garnished with additional parsley. Makes 8 to 10 servings.

BEAN SOUP

2   cups dried navy beans
½   cup lentils
2   quarts water
1   large cooked ham bone with some meat still on it
    Salt and pepper to taste
3   tablespoons butter
½   cup chopped onion (optional)

Wash beans and lentils, place in soup kettle, cover with water and soak overnight. (Short method: wash, cover with water, bring to a boil, let soak one hour.) Drain. Add 2 quarts water and ham bone. Bring to a boil, lower heat and simmer until beans are soft, stirring occasionally to prevent scorching. Remove bone when beans are soft. Pick meat from bone and return to pot. Season with salt and pepper. Add butter. One-half cup chopped onion may be added during simmering if desired.

MOLASSES COOKIES

½ pound light brown sugar
1 cup margarine or butter
2 cups dark molasses
2 cups buttermilk or sour milk
6 cups flour
1 tablespoon baking soda
1 teaspoon ginger
1 teaspoon cinnamon

Cream together sugar and margarine or butter. Add molasses and milk. Stir in flour, baking soda and spices. Drop by large spoonfuls onto cookie sheet. Bake at 375 degrees for 8 to 10 minutes. Makes 8 dozen.

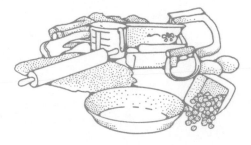

SHOO FLY PIE

1 9" unbaked pie shell
1 cup flour
1 tablespoon margarine
  or butter
⅔ cup brown sugar
½ teaspoon salt
3 tablespoons ice water

1 egg, slightly beaten
1 cup dark molasses
1 cup boiling water, divided
1 tablespoon baking soda

Make crumb mixture by cutting together 1 cup flour, margarine or butter, and brown sugar. Set aside ½ cup of this mixture for topping. To remaining crumb mixture add egg and molasses. Add ¾ cup boiling water to molasses mixture. Dissolve baking soda in remaining ¼ cup boiling water and add to molasses mixture. Pour into prepared pie shell. Top with reserved crumbs. Bake at 425 degrees for 15 minutes. Reduce oven to 350 degrees and bake 45 minutes longer.

HENRY EDWARDS HUNTINGTON

HENRY EDWARDS HUNTINGTON (1850-1927) amassed a fortune through his interests in railroad companies and real estate holdings in Southern California.

His wide range of interests is displayed at the Huntington Library in San Marino, California, which was once his home. This magnificent 206-acre estate contains one of the finest libraries in the world, a splendid collection of British art which includes Gainsborough's "Blue Boy" and Lawrence's "Pinky," and botanical gardens covering more than 130 acres.

At his home in San Marino, Huntington collected plants for their ornamental as well as agricultural value, and engaged in experiments to determine which of the world's plants would thrive in Southern California. It is said that when Huntington first tasted an avocado at his dining club, he was so intrigued that he pocketed the huge pit and had it planted in his garden of exotica. There, so Californians say, the same plant bears fruit today. Huntington's continuing efforts led to his becoming the first commercial grower of the now ubiquitous avocado, which is featured in the following recipes.

GUACAMOLE

2   avocados
1   chopped tomato
½   minced onion
1   tablespoon lime or lemon juice
¼   teaspoon garlic salt
    Salt and pepper

If the avocados are hard when you buy them in the store, allow them to ripen (not in the refrigerator!) until they begin to feel a little bit soft to the touch. Cut them in half, remove stones, peel, and mash up the avocado meat with the rest of the ingredients. Use as a party dip with corn chips or tortilla chips, or use as a garnish on any salad. Dabs of guacamole may be topped with a teaspoonful of sour cream sprinkled with paprika for added decoration.

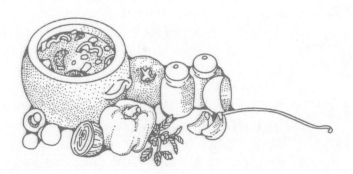

Avocado Curry Soup

1 tablespoon butter
1 teaspoon curry
1¼ cups chicken consommé
1 cup cream
1 slightly beaten egg yolk
1 medium-size avocado, peeled and seeded

Melt butter, stir in curry and add consommé. Bring to boil; cover and simmer 10 minutes. Combine cream with egg yolk and gradually stir into the soup. Mash half the avocado; dice the other half; add both to the soup. Heat, stirring constantly. Serve hot or cold. Serves 5.

Chicken and Avocado Salad

3 avocados
Fresh lemon juice
Salt
2 cups chicken, cooked and cubed
1½ cups celery, diced
½ cup toasted almonds, slivered
1 cup mayonnaise
1 teaspoon mustard

Halve, seed and peel avocados. Sprinkle with lemon juice and salt. Combine chicken, celery, almonds, mayonnaise and mustard. Top avocado halves with chicken mixture, Serves 6.

JOSEPH P. KENNEDY AND JOHN F. KENNEDY

JOSEPH P. KENNEDY (1888-1969), a prominent businessman and financier, made millions on Wall Street, in Hollywood, in real estate, and in other endeavors. This wealth, some of which was accumulated in questionable ventures, enabled him to give his children everything.

As a young man, Joseph P. Kennedy liked home cooking of the New England variety, often coming home from Harvard on Sundays and bringing friends to feast on his mother's baked ham and beans. While his children were growing up, their education in politics and world affairs took place around the dining table during formal dinners.

John Fitzgerald Kennedy (1917-1963), Joseph P. Kennedy's second son, was in 1960 elected 35th President of the United States, overcoming the once strong anti-Catholic feelings in the country which his father had seen as a stumbling block.

John F. Kennedy was a light eater, and had his father's taste for New England cooking, with fish chowder a special favorite. According to one of his White House chefs, his favorite dinner was lamb chops, mashed potatoes, tossed salad with a special bleu cheese dressing, strawberry tarts, and coffee. Some of the recipes used in the Kennedy White House appear below.

BLEU CHEESE DRESSING

  1 cup mayonnaise
3½ tablespoons vinegar
 ½ cup sour cream
  6 ounces bleu cheese
 ¾ cup milk
 ½ teaspoon salt

Beat all ingredients together until thoroughly blended, or place everything in a blender and blend until smooth and creamy. Makes a little more than 1 pint.

NEW ENGLAND FISH CHOWDER

2 pounds haddock
2 cups water
2 ounces salt pork, diced
2 onions, sliced
4 large potatoes, diced
1 cup chopped celery
1 bay leaf, crumbled
1 teaspoon salt
   Freshly ground black pepper
1 quart milk
2 tablespoons butter

Simmer the haddock in the water for 15 minutes. Drain. Reserve the broth. Remove the bones from the fish. Saute the pork until crisp, remove from pan, and set aside. Saute the onions in the pork fat until golden brown. Add the fish, potatoes, celery, bay leaf, salt, and pepper. Pour in fish broth, plus enough boiling water to make 3 cups liquid. Simmer for 30 minutes. Add the milk and butter, and simmer for 5 minutes. Serve the chowder sprinkled with pork dice. Serves 6.

BAKED BEANS

4 cups dry pea beans
1 small onion, chopped
¼ pound salt pork, diced
¾ cup brown sugar or molasses
½ cup catsup
1 teaspoon dry mustard
2 teaspoons salt
1 tablespoon Worcestershire sauce
1 cup boiling water
¼ pound salt pork, cut into strips

Cover the pea beans with water. Bring slowly to a boil, or soak overnight. Drain. Cover with fresh water, and simmer slowly. When the skins of the beans start to burst open, the beans are sufficiently cooked. Drain and add onion, diced salt pork, sugar or molasses, catsup, mustard, salt, Worcestershire sauce, and boiling water.

Place in a greased casserole dish, and decorate top with salt pork strips. Bake, covered, in a very slow oven 6 to 8 hours. Uncover for the last hour of cooking. Add more water or stock if the beans become dry. Serves 12 to 16.

Above recipes reprinted with permission of Collier Associates from A Treasury of White House Cooking *by Francois Rysavy as told to Frances Spatz Leighton (G.P. Putnam's Sons, New York, 1972).*

ESTÉE LAUDER

ESTÉE LAUDER, whose age has never been
disclosed, is the founder of a cosmetics
conglomerate that she built with style and
marketing acumen into an empire. Her creams,
perfumes and makeup are sold to men and
women all over the world.

Estée Lauder is not only a successful
entrepreneur but also a renowned hostess, and
has entertained such celebrities as the Duke
and Duchess of Windsor, Princess Grace of
Monaco, and Douglas Fairbanks.

She supervises every aspect of a party and
still makes it appear effortless. Lighting sets
the mood, often by use of a multitude of
candles, and the table glitters with either gold
or silver accessories. Instead of tall flower
centerpieces, small antique silver tankards
may be used, filled perhaps with lilies of the
valley. Fresh fruits and vegetables are also
used decoratively, and music is an important
part of every party.

One of Estée Lauder's helpful party tips is
to cook an extraordinary first course and
dessert. In-between courses may be catered,
but it is the beginning and end that people will
remember best.

Some suggestions for a festive dinner
party follow. The recipes have been adapted
by the editor from the suggested menu.

FIRST COURSE

Cold jellied borscht with a dollop of sour cream and
a teaspoon of fresh caviar on top
or
Not-too-thick or not-too-thin vegetable soup with
delicate crackers
or
Fresh crabmeat in cream sauce

MAIN COURSE

Crown roast of lamb
or
Whole poached salmon garnished with thin slices of
cucumber and lemon served with a dill sauce
or
Stuffed baked squab with a side dressing of guava
jelly served in a ring of wild rice with hearts of
artichokes and tiny fresh mushrooms

SALAD

A mixture of endive, watercress and white seedless
grapes

DESSERT

Warmed rhubarb and strawberry pie
or
Pears in wine

IRISH COFFEE

PEARS POACHED IN WINE

6 or 8   Bosc pears, peeled, with stems intact
   1   cinnamon stick
   2   cups red wine
  ½   cup sugar
   4   tablespoons lemon juice
       Vanilla ice cream, softened
       Slivers of bittersweet chocolate, grated

Slowly simmer pears with cinnamon stick in wine, sugar, and lemon juice for about 45 minutes or until pears are tender but definitely whole. Leave pears to cool in the wine mixture at room temperature. Spoon softened ice cream into a crystal bowl and stand the pears around the edge of the bowl, stem up. Sprinkle chocolate over ice cream. Serves 6-8.

POACHED SALMON

Remove head and tail from salmon. Wash fish and pat dry with a paper towel. Place salmon in a poacher and cover with court bouillon. Simmer 8 minutes per pound. Remove from poacher and skin the fish. Garnish with lemon slices and cucumber. Serve either hot or cold with a dill sauce.

ANDREW W. MELLON

ANDREW W. MELLON (1855-1937) was a giant
among businessmen, perhaps one of the
greatest in the country's history. He founded
and backed a number of companies including
Aluminum Company of America and Gulf Oil
Corporation, and helped develop what is now
known as the Mellon Bank Corporation.
(Mellon, a reticent man, felt most comfortable
at the Bank.) He also served as Secretary of
the Treasury under Presidents Harding,
Coolidge and Hoover.

Mellon loved Pittsburgh, where he was
born and educated. Until leaving for
Washington in 1921, he lunched almost daily at
Pittsburgh's Duquesne Club. Mellon was so
diffident that he had his chauffeur drop him off
a block from the Club, enabling him to make
an unobtrusive entrance The Duquesne Club
Maitre D', Steve Schultz, and the Club Wine
Steward (both now retired) remember Mellon
as a diner who was generally easy to please.
Schultz recalls that Mellon frequently chose
either lamb hash or a club sandwich for lunch.
Recipes for these dishes follow.

LAMB HASH WITH POACHED EGG AND TOMATO SAUCE

2   pounds cooked leg of lamb, cut into small cubes
1   medium onion, diced fine
1   green pepper, diced fine
4   cloves garlic, minced
1   bay leaf
2   ounces sherry wine
5-6 ounces brown sauce
1   tablespoon chopped parsley
2   tablespoons crushed black pepper
    Salt to taste
6   medium potatoes, cooked, cut into small cubes
6   poached eggs
6   ounces tomato sauce

Braise lamb, onion, green pepper, and garlic in a
casserole in a 400-degree oven. Cook until fat has
been rendered. Then add sherry wine, brown sauce
and bay leaf. Braise again for 10-15 minutes, then add
the black pepper, salt and parsley. Braise again for
10-15 minutes. Add cubed potatoes. If hash remains
thin, add a small amount of bread crumbs until
mixture is tight enough to be rolled. Divide into 6
portions and brown each in a very hot omelet pan.
Garnish each individual hash portion with a freshly
made poached egg. Also, a small amount of tomato
sauce can be used as a bed for each portion. Serves 6.

Above recipe provided by the Duquesne Club

Classic Turkey Club Sandwich

3 large square slices of toasted white bread
   Butter, mayonnaise or Russian dressing
   Lettuce
3 crisp slices hot bacon
   Tomato slices
   Cold cooked turkey, sliced

Spread toast on one side only with butter, mayonnaise or Russian dressing. Cover the spread side of first slice of toast with lettuce leaf, bacon, and tomato slices. On top of this place second slice of toast, spread side up, and cover with sliced turkey. Place third slice of toast on top, spread side down, and cut sandwich in halves or quarters.

J. P. MORGAN

JOHN PIERPONT MORGAN (1837-1913) was the founder of J.P. Morgan & Company, the most prosperous banking house in the country, and organized the world's largest corporation, United States Steel. He reorganized groups of railroads into such transportation giants as the Chesapeake & Ohio and Northern Pacific, and was involved in the formation of General Electric and International Harvester. Morgan's financial interests did not occupy all of his time, however; he was also an avid collector of books and manuscripts.

The Morgan Library on 36th Street in New York is a magnificent legacy to the American public from a man who loved literature and beautiful works of art. His enjoyment of the better things in life extended to good food, evidenced by his membership in an elite social dining club called the Zodiac Club, which met at members' homes or at a club.

J.P. Morgan cared nothing for balls, cotillions, gilt chairs or chatter. He preferred solid comforts, and people much like himself.

The members of the Zodiac Club competed in producing sumptuous meals, of as many as six, eight or ten courses, meant to be eaten from start to finish. Following is a menu of a dinner held by the eating club at the University Club in New York.

Menu.

Amontillado Sherry
Cotuit oysters
Bisque of Crabs à la Norfolk
Consommé de volaille Sévigné
Hors-d'oeuvres variés
Rhine Wine, 1893
Soft Clams à l'ancienne
Chateau-Latour, 1878
Saddle and rack of spring lamb
Mint sauce
Peas à la Francaise
Bermuda potatoes rissolées
Moet & Chandon, 1893
Terrapin, Maryland Club
Grapefruit au Kirsch
Clos-Vougeot, 1893
Canvasback ducks
Fried hominy
Celery à l'université
Parfait noisettes
Cheese
Fruit
Coffee
Cognac, 1805

Reprinted from J. Pierpont Morgan: An Intimate Portrait *by Herbert L. Satterlee (The Macmillan Company, New York, 1940).*

Sevigny Consommé

1 chicken, quartered
1 veal shank
1 tablespoon butter
1 onion, quartered
4 quarts water
1 bay leaf
6 cloves
3 peppercorns
2 egg whites

Braise chicken, veal shank and onion in butter. Place chicken, veal and onion in stewing pot and add water, bay leaf, cloves and peppercorns. Simmer for 3 hours. Add ¼ cup of stock to braising pan and glaze. Return glaze to stewing pot. Strain stock and remove fat. Clarify stock by adding the egg whites. Boil again and strain through a broth napkin. Serves 8.

Ethel Mills

HENRY PHIPPS

HENRY PHIPPS (1837-1930) was born in Philadelphia and grew up in Pittsburgh. Like many of his famous contemporaries, he left school at an early age to go to work, continuing his education later in night school and in private study while working as a bookkeeper for D. W. C. Bidwell & Co. (where he eventually became a partner). In the early 1860's he entered into the iron business with Andrew Kloman and then shortly afterward with Andrew and Thomas M. Carnegie as well, in time becoming a multi-millionäire.

The Phipps conservatories in Schenley Park in Pittsburgh and in Allegheny were donated by Phipps for the use of the public. He also gave Pittsburgh a botanical school, and founded the Phipps Institute in Philadelphia to war on tuberculosis.

Phipps, like the Mellons and the Carnegies, was a member of the prestigious Duquesne Club where, on December 10, 1909, a number of friends and former associates honored Phipps with an elegant dinner, the menu of which follows:

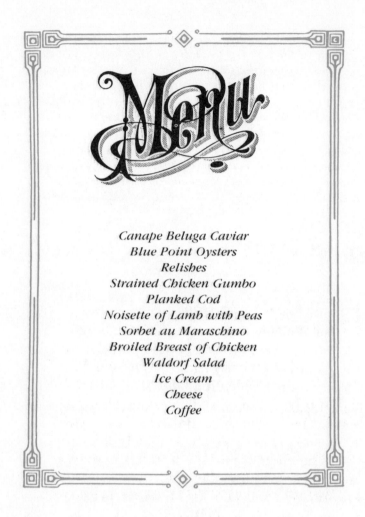

Menu

Canape Beluga Caviar
Blue Point Oysters
Relishes
Strained Chicken Gumbo
Planked Cod
Noisette of Lamb with Peas
Sorbet au Maraschino
Broiled Breast of Chicken
Waldorf Salad
Ice Cream
Cheese
Coffee

Oysters

*Oysters should be kept in a very cold place, and be
thoroughly washed before they are opened; they should,
according to the French custom, be opened on the deep
shell so as to preserve their liquor. It is then advisable,
if possible, to lay them on a bed of finely-chopped ice
for an hour or so before serving; this improves the
flavour greatly, but they must not be left on the ice
much longer, for after that time they will begin to lose
flavour, instead of gaining it.*

*To open an Oyster it should be held in the folds of
a cloth, in the palm of the hand, or in a hollow cut out
of a piece of wood; an Oyster-knife can then be inserted
between the shells with a see-saw motion, forcing it
inwards and cutting the Oyster away from the flat
shell. When the knife has done its work the flat shell
can be removed. In most cases it is usual to remove the
beards or "fringes" of the oysters before using them for
cooking; but that is not an absolute necessity, although
advisable. After cutting the body loose from the deep
shell, they are then ready to serve or use as may be
required.*

From The Encyclopedia of Practical Cookery *(19th C., England).*

SAUCE FOR OYSTERS ON THE HALF SHELL

⅛ cup prepared horseradish
4 tablespoons tomato ketchup
½ teaspoon salt
2 tablespoons vinegar
4 tablespoons lemon juice
¼ teaspoon Tabasco

Combine all ingredients and serve with fresh cold
oysters on the half shell. Oysters should be placed on
a bed of crushed ice.

JOHN D. ROCKEFELLER

JOHN D. ROCKEFELLER, the noted industrialist
and philanthropist, was born in 1839 and
died in 1937 at age 97. He built up the
Standard Oil Trust which, in 1890 when the
Sherman Anti-Trust Act was passed, controlled
95% of the petroleum refining industry.
Rockefeller also had extensive holdings in
mining, manufacturing, and transportation.

In his later years, Rockefeller lived simply
at his home in Pocantico Hills, New York, a
magnificent estate of 3,000 acres. He rose
early, took a morning walk, read the papers
thoroughly and by about ten was playing golf.
After bathing, a noon lunch and a short nap,
Rockefeller spent the afternoon on business
and usually took a ride in the Peerless
automobile which he used for 15 years. He
dined promptly at 7:30, dressed formally, and
sat at the table for a full hour, usually with
guests, although he ate little.

Rockefeller was not above uttering words
of wisdom on mundane subjects. Once, passing
a group of young women at a heaping Sunday
School picnic table, he remarked: "Remember,
girls, if you eat slowly, you can eat more!"

His advice to Andrew Carnegie was
similar. Upon receiving some oatmeal from
Carnegie, Rockefeller responded in this
manner:

4 West Fifty-fourth Street
February 2, 1903.

My Dear Mr. Carnegie:

I thank you for the oatmeal of your own manufacture, which you were kind enough to send me. It is very good and I hope you enjoy the eating of it as much as I do. Be sure to eat it very slowly and masticate well.

You grind oatmeal: I grind apples, and have ordered a bottle of my sweet cider sent you from Pocantico.

Keep right on with your grand work of giving away money, regardless of the criticisms of cranks and fools. You have already given away more money than any man living.

The good Lord bless you and give you wisdom for your great responsibilities.

Very sincerely yours,

Jno. D. Rockefeller

Apple Cider

Wash thoroughly fully ripened apples and remove all leaves. Using a clean press, extract the juice from the crushed apples. Boil juice in a large open preserving kettle until only half of liquid remains. Skim often. Pour into hot sterilized jars and seal at once.

Oysters Rockefeller was invented at Antoine's in New Orleans at the turn of the century. The dish was named for Rockefeller because it was incredibly rich.

Oysters Rockefeller

36 oysters on the half shell
    Rock salt
2 cups cooked and drained spinach
¼ cup chopped scallions
2 tablespoons minced parsley
2 tablespoons finely chopped celery
½ teaspoon salt
6 drops hot pepper sauce
⅓ cup butter
2 teaspoons anisette
½ cup fine dried bread crumbs

Put oysters in their shells on a bed of rock salt so they will remain upright and not lose their juice. Combine spinach, scallions, parsley and celery. Put this mixture through a food grinder. Add salt and hot pepper sauce, mixing well. Cook mixture in butter and anisette over low heat for 4 or 5 minutes. Fold in bread crumbs and spread 1 tablespoon of mixture on each oyster. Bake in a 400 degree oven for 10 minutes or until lightly browned.

CAROLINE HUNT SCHOELLKOPF

DAUGHTER OF MULTI-BILLIONAIRE OIL MAGNATE
H.L. Hunt and reputed to be one of
America's richest women, Caroline Hunt
Schoellkopf (who is now in her 60's) is a wife
and mother of five grown children, and has
found time to be active in religious, cultural
and civic affairs.

She was the first woman deacon of the
Highland Park Presbyterian Church, has served
as a trustee of Mary Baldwin College in
Staunton, Virginia, and has donated historically
significant structures to the Dallas County
Heritage Society's Old City Park. She serves on
the boards of a number of charitable
organizations including the Salvation Army,
Dallas Symphony League, and the Kennedy
Center. Mrs. Schoellkopf has no live-in help,
does her own shopping and her own hair, and
cooks dinners herself.

In 1980 Mrs. Schoellkopf authored a 440-
recipe pumpkin cookbook entitled "The
Compleat Pumpkin Eater" for her husband's
helicopter charter service (which in her honor
is called "Pumpkin Air"). The recipes that
follow are from this book, except for the
pumpkin almond bisque that won first place
for Mrs. Schoellkopf in the 1983 Gourmet Gala
in Houston.

Pumpkin Almond Bisque in Its Own Shell

2 tablespoons butter
3 tablespoons chopped celery
3 tablespoons chopped onion
2 cups cooked pumpkin puree
1 tablespoon tomato paste
2 tablespoons almond paste
3 cups chicken broth
1½ cups light cream
1 teaspoon nutmeg
1 teaspoon white pepper
3 tablespoons amaretto
Salt to taste
Toasted pumpkin seeds (Pepitas) as garnish

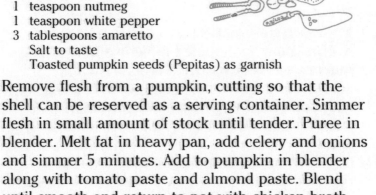

Remove flesh from a pumpkin, cutting so that the shell can be reserved as a serving container. Simmer flesh in small amount of stock until tender. Puree in blender. Melt fat in heavy pan, add celery and onions and simmer 5 minutes. Add to pumpkin in blender along with tomato paste and almond paste. Blend until smooth and return to pot with chicken broth and simmer 30 minutes. Blend the cream into the soup. Cook until hot. Season with nutmeg, pepper, salt and amaretto. Serve in pumpkin shell and float toasted pumpkin seeds on each serving.

Pepitas

Remove seeds from pumpkin and separate from fibers. Cover with salted water and simmer for one hour. Drain and dry on brown paper. (This step unnecessary with naked or hulless seeds such as Lady Godiva.) Coat with oil in which has been mixed 2 tablespoons Worcestershire sauce, ¼ teaspoon cayenne pepper and 1 teaspoon salt. Stir from time to time while baking in a 275 degree oven until golden brown. May be eaten with or without hulls. Add 2 tablespoons curry powder if desired.

SOUR CREAM PUMPKIN PIE

1½ cups cooked pureed pumpkin
3 egg yolks, beaten
1 cup packed brown sugar
½ teaspoon salt
½ teaspoon powdered ginger
½ teaspoon cinnamon
1½ cups sour cream
2 tablespoons grated orange rind
3 egg whites
1 9" pastry shell, baked 10 minutes and cooled

In a bowl, beat together the pumpkin, egg yolks, sugar, salt, ginger and cinnamon. Gradually mix in the sour cream. Pour into the top of a double boiler; place over hot water and cook, stirring constantly, until thickened. Cool 15 minutes. Pour into the pre-baked pie shell. Top with egg whites which have been stiffly beaten with the orange peel added the last minute of beating. Place in a 400 degree oven and heat until the meringue is browned. May be served warm or cooled.

PUMPKIN DATE BREAD

¾ cup salad oil
1 cup sugar
2 eggs, beaten
2 cups grated pumpkin
1½ cups sifted flour
1 teaspoon baking soda
1 teaspoon cinnamon
½ teaspoon salt
1 cup chopped nuts (optional)
1 cup raisins
1 cup chopped dates

Combine all ingredients in order listed. Mix well. Pour batter into one 9" x 5" x 3" greased and floured loaf pan or two 7" x 3" x 2" greased and floured loaf pans. Bake at 350 degrees for 1 hour or until bread tests done. Makes 1 large or 2 small loaves.

COMMODORE VANDERBILT

CORNELIUS "COMMODORE" VANDERBILT (1794-1877) commanded a line of seagoing vessels and the New York Central and other railroads, accumulating an estimated $100 million fortune by his death. During the panic of 1873 he ordered the construction of Grand Central Terminal in New York City, providing jobs to thousands of unemployed.

In the 1850's Commodore Vanderbilt was a frequent visitor to Saratoga, New York, the well-known spa and racing center. Legend has it that one evening in 1853 Vanderbilt dined at Moon's Lake House at Saratoga Lake. He rejected a batch of french fried potatoes because they were too thick. The chef, in revenge, sliced some potatoes very thin, fried them to a crisp, and salted them heavily. Much to the chef's surprise, Vanderbilt loved them, as did subsequent guests at the restaurant, and thus began the "Saratoga Chip," later to become known as the potato chip.

These recipes using potato chips were graciously provided by Mrs. Cornelius Vanderbilt Whitney from her book, "The Potato Chip Cookbook," and are slightly adapted from the original.

Chip Burgers

1½   pounds ground round steak or hamburger
½   cup chopped onion
    Pepper
1   cup crushed potato chips

Mix the ground meat with the onion and pepper. Add the crushed potato chips and mix. Make into patties. Should make 6 large hamburgers. Cook on grill or in frying pan. Serves 6.

Chicken Dip

½   cup minced chicken (cooked)
½   cup mayonnaise
½   cup sour cream
¼   cup curry powder
    Pepper

Mix all together and serve as a dip with potato chips.

Oyster Dip

1 large size package cream cheese
2 tablespoons cream
1 teaspoon grated onion
1 tablespoon chopped parsley
2 tablespoons of dry sherry
1 jar or tin of drained smoked oysters

Chopped oysters are preferable. If whole, they must be chopped fine. Soften cream cheese with cream and mix with oysters, sherry, parsley and onion. Serve as a dip with chips.

Chick 'n Chip Casserole

2 cups of diced cooked chicken
2 stalks celery, diced
¾ cup mayonnaise
1 tablespoon finely chopped onion
½ lemon, juiced
½ cup grated mild cheddar cheese
1 cup crushed potato chips

Combine chicken, celery, mayonnaise, onion, and lemon juice. Pour into a casserole. Sprinkle with the cheese and then top with potato chips. Bake in a 425 degree oven for 20 to 30 minutes. Serves 6.

GEORGE WASHINGTON VANDERBILT

GEORGE WASHINGTON VANDERBILT (1862-1914) was the grandson of Cornelius "Commodore" Vanderbilt, the financier and railroad magnate. He was the son of William Henry Vanderbilt, who doubled the family fortune, thus providing his heirs with the means to create some of the most palatial residences of the gilded age.

In 1889 George Washington Vanderbilt bought 125,000 acres of land near Asheville, North Carolina, on which he built a magnificent 250-room mansion called Biltmore. Here he carried on extensive experiments in stock breeding and scientific farming. The house made use of all the latest technology, including electric dumbwaiters, walk-in refrigerators and an electrically turned roasting spit on which game was prepared.

In this French Renaissance chateau, elegant meals were served on monogrammed Minton and Spode china and beverages were poured into Baccarat crystal, in the banquet hall under vaulted ceiling arches 70 feet high.

A menu from a dinner served to Mr. Vanderbilt in New York gives the reader an idea of the richness and abundance of the food served at Biltmore during its heyday.

March 26, 1892

Blue Points
Celery   Olives   Radishes
Salted Almonds
Saucie de Lyon
Consommé Royale
Broiled Shad
Parisienne Potatoes
Cucumber Salad
Terrapin a la Maryland
Sweet Bread with French Peas
Sorbet
Snow Birds
Lettuce Salad
Cheese and Biscuit
Ice Cream
Fruit—Coffee

Menu provided by the Biltmore
Estate, Asheville, North Carolina.

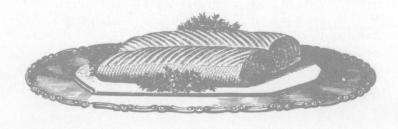

Broiled Shad

Scale and clean a large Shad, remove the fins, and score it on both sides. Put the fish in a deep dish with some chopped shallots, parsley, salt, and oil, and let it macerate for one hour. Grease a gridiron, warm it, and lay the fish on it; broil the Shad over a clear fire, turning it occasionally and basting with oil. The Shad will take from half-an-hour to three-quarters-of-an hour to cook, according to its size. When ready, put the fish on a folded napkin on a hot dish, garnish with parsley, and serve with a sauceboatful of maitre d'hotel sauce.

The fish is split so as not to come in halves, and made to lie flat on the gridiron, which must be previously greased and heated. Sprinkle the fish plentifully with pepper and salt, and when it is put upon the dish, pour over it a little warmed butter, and garnish with fried parsley.

From The Encyclopedia of Practical Cookery *(19th C., England).*

BROILED SHAD AND ROE

1   3-pound shad, boned
1   shad roe
½   pound mushrooms, sliced
     Salt and pepper
¼   cup melted butter
1   tablespoon fresh lemon juice
2   tablespoons white wine
     Parsley

Preheat broiler. Remove head and tail from shad; cut into 5 serving pieces. Arrange with skin side down on lightly greased broiler pan, with roe and mushrooms around fish. Season with salt and pepper. Brush fish with some butter and lemon juice. Broil fish 2 inches from heat for 10 minutes. Baste with butter occasionally. After 4 minutes turn roe and mushrooms. When ready to serve sprinkle with wine and parsley. Serves 5.

Index